Making Birds, Beasts and Insects

Barbara Snook

Charles Scribner's Sons
New York

Contents

Acknowledgment

Materials for making *Birds, Beasts and Insects* has been collected over the years. Some of the creatures were made by students and wherever possible their work has been acknowledged. My most grateful thanks are given to Mr Samuel Carr for persuading me to attempt a successor to *Clowns, Witches and Dragons* and to Thelma M Nye for once again being such a skilful editor.

Eastbourne 1974   *B L S*

Introduction

A few toys have found their way into this miscellaneous collection: Apart from these none of the other work was intended to last, though when construction was sound and the chosen materials did not decay a few survived quite a long time. Generally, in creative work of this kind, the joy is in the discovery and immediate use of odd ingredients and the way in which they combine to give sometimes unexpected results.

All manner of things can be used and the majority can be joined with rubber based adhesives which have the great advantage of drying transparent, if not in being completely invisible.

Certainly some materials are easier than others to handle. Bones, of animal, poultry and fish, call for a great deal of patience in the initial stages, for they must be boiled absolutely clean and be completely dry before they are fit to use.

Given a certain amount of ingenuity and a roving eye for likely specimens, ideas soon take shape. Old pieces of wood and bark collected on country walks or rescued from a garden bonfire often resemble animal and bird forms so closely that hardly any additional material is needed.

Walks along the sea shore at low tide can provide worthwhile flotsam and jetsam, but beware, seaweed, attractive though it is, very soon becomes smelly. Clean white cuttlefish bone often found cast up on the shingle can be carved and painted and is soft enough to allow things to be stabbed into it.

Seashore, garden and countryside give much treasure trove to add to that found at home. If the specimens are completely dry they can be stored in a box, but be careful, anything slightly damp may turn the whole collection mouldy in a very short time and make the would-be sculptor unpopular.

Pipe cleaner ostrich

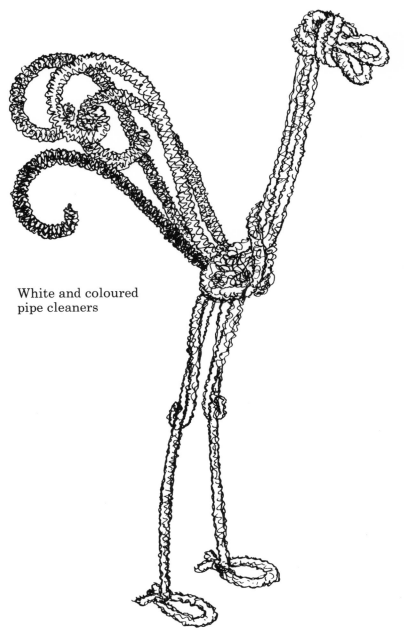

White and coloured
pipe cleaners

Cream carton crane

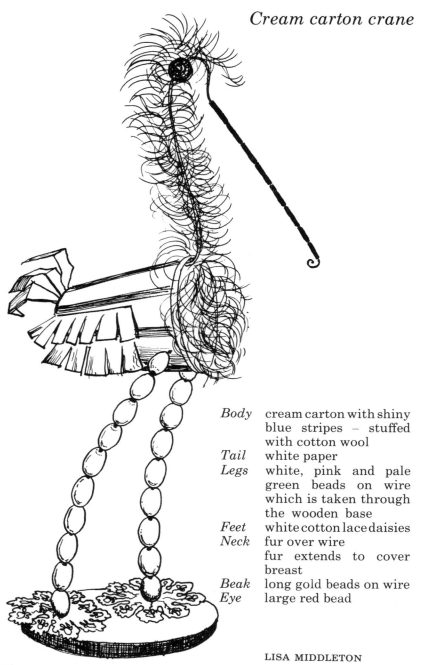

Body	cream carton with shiny blue stripes – stuffed with cotton wool
Tail	white paper
Legs	white, pink and pale green beads on wire which is taken through the wooden base
Feet	white cotton lace daisies
Neck	fur over wire fur extends to cover breast
Beak	long gold beads on wire
Eye	large red bead

LISA MIDDLETON

Crested heron

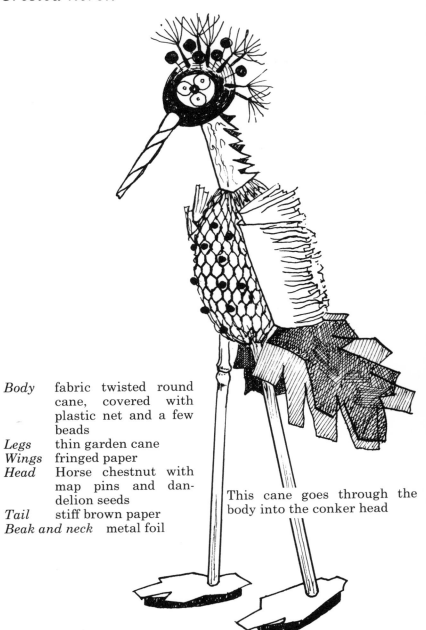

Body	fabric twisted round cane, covered with plastic net and a few beads
Legs	thin garden cane
Wings	fringed paper
Head	Horse chestnut with map pins and dandelion seeds
Tail	stiff brown paper
Beak and neck	metal foil

This cane goes through the body into the conker head

Fluffy chick

Head	piece of egg carton covered with teazed out wools	*Feet*	shells
		Neck and legs	wire, wrapped with silver paper
Eyes	buttons	*Body and wings*	fur
Beak	felt		
Tail	large feather decorations with fluffy feathers	Standing on a moss-tufted rubber plant leaf	

Fir cone bird

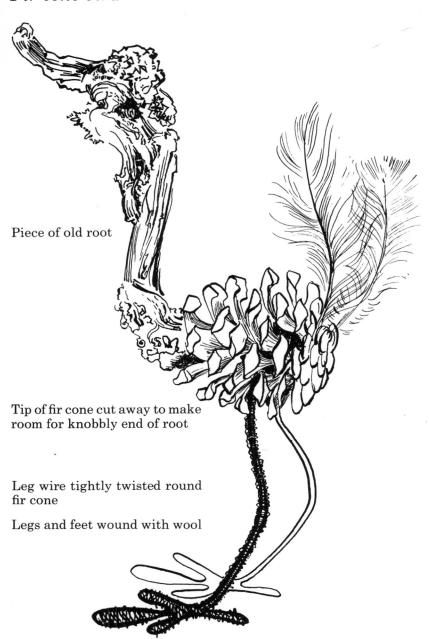

Piece of old root

Tip of fir cone cut away to make
room for knobbly end of root

Leg wire tightly twisted round
fir cone

Legs and feet wound with wool

Made from pig's jaw bone and small bone from skull joined with *Polyfiller*

Wing and ruff	plastic vegetable net
Chick's head	sunflower seeds stuck on to pig's teeth
Head bone	opposite side, actual size

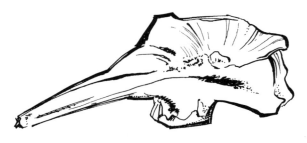

This side gives a natural crest but a smaller eye

Paper cone bird

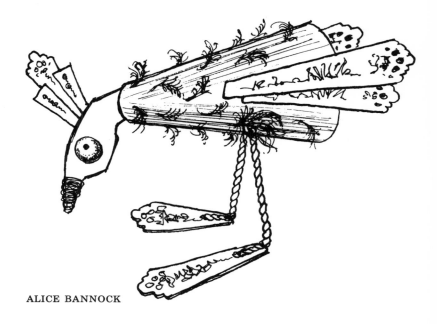

ALICE BANNOCK

Eyes   large pearl beads
Body   paper cone with small feathers, an ice cream cone could be used but would be fragile
Head   several thicknesses of thin card
Crest, wings and feet   pieces of a toy fan
Legs   wire covered with paper the wire is taken through the body

Onion bird

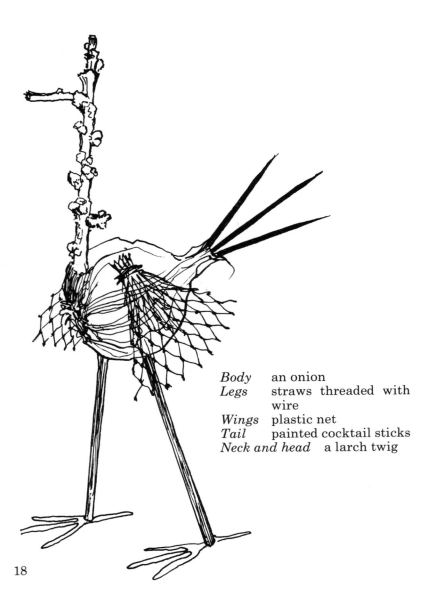

Body an onion
Legs straws threaded with wire
Wings plastic net
Tail painted cocktail sticks
Neck and head a larch twig

Plaited straw bird

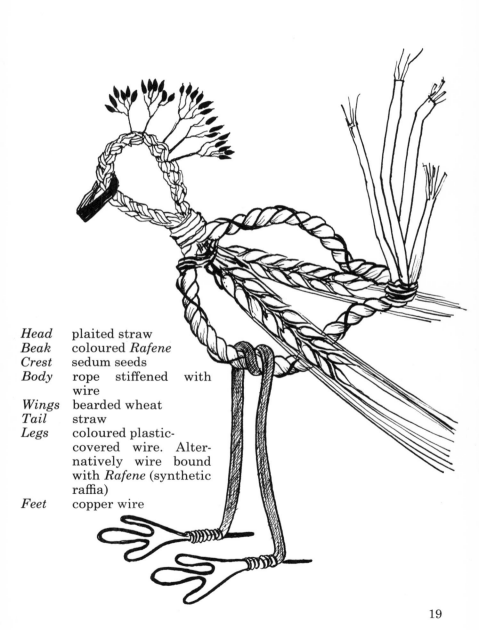

Head	plaited straw
Beak	coloured *Rafene*
Crest	sedum seeds
Body	rope stiffened with wire
Wings	bearded wheat
Tail	straw
Legs	coloured plastic-covered wire. Alternatively wire bound with *Rafene* (synthetic raffia)
Feet	copper wire

Bark bird

To be seen from one side only

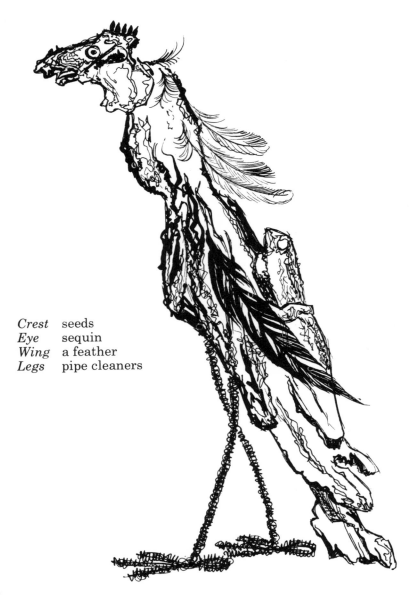

Crest	seeds
Eye	sequin
Wing	a feather
Legs	pipe cleaners

20

Duck in flight

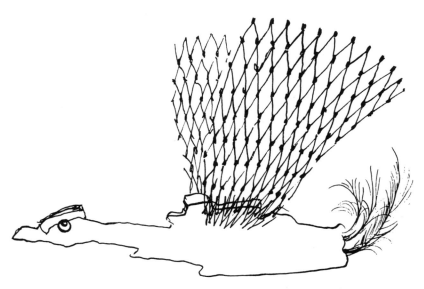

Bark

Plastic net wings and tail

Bead eyes

Fuse wire to keep wings in shape

Tail can be a sweet cup paper if available

The roughness of bark may make it difficult to find a surface for sticking on decoration. *Plastic wood* or *Polyfiller* will help

STEPHANIE HAY

Ostrich

*which, with a different tail
and two more legs becomes a
giraffe*

Peach stone duck

Body   very old, weathered peach stone found in garden, it needed hard scrubbing before use

Head   beech husk filled with snipped felt. The stem forms the beak

Eye   a bead

The same peach stone seen from the other side

Head   beech husk. If the felt neck is inserted carefully the dark hollow looks like an eye

Neck   roll of felt over wire. Edges glued to stone

Feet   felt

Crest   pine needles

Head   orange cape-gooseberry husk

Beak   a blackthorn spine

Eye   berry from inside the husk

Neck and body   thick wire with 3 beads and face-to-face wooden button moulds in graduated sizes

Wings   coloured cellophane over wire which is tightly twisted round body wire

Legs   a continuous piece of wire, each loop having been pinched with pliers

Feet   wound with wool

Toes   sealing wax

Tail   thin metal – coffee tin seal

Cape gooseberry bird

Twist wires tightly to make
wings and legs rigid

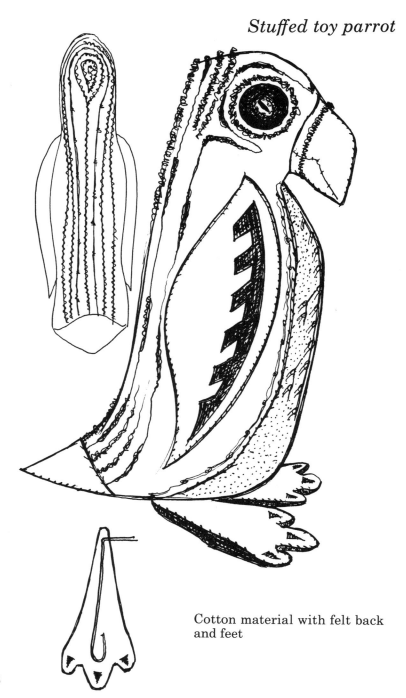

Cotton material with felt back and feet

Stuffed toy vulture

Materials	silk and cotton
Beak	felt
Feet	padded felt over wire
	Net frills

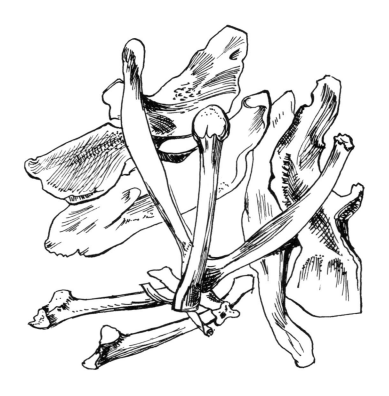

MARY CRUST

Onion headed bristle bird

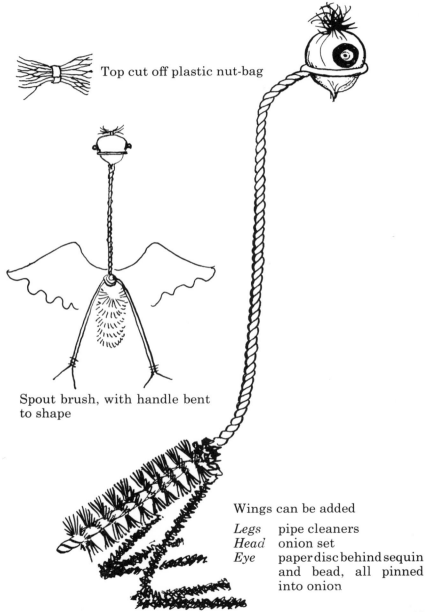

Top cut off plastic nut-bag

Spout brush, with handle bent to shape

Wings can be added

Legs pipe cleaners
Head onion set
Eye paper disc behind sequin and bead, all pinned into onion

Piece of old root – this side had
black bark

Head ripe cupressus cone
Eyes orange berries from iris
        foetida
Ears felt
Tail plaited raffia

Old root squirrel

The same root from the opposite side

Tail golden rod seeds

Head a lump of modelling cement into which eucalyptus seed eyes were pressed

Ears velvet with wool tufts, set into modelling cement

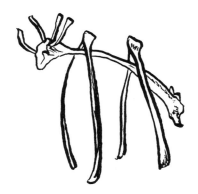

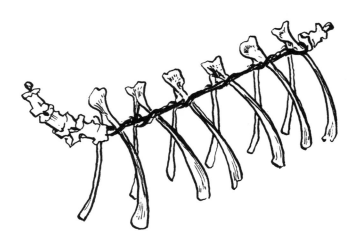

Animals made from chicken ribs and small vertebrae. Bones joined together with PV glue

Curtain-spring cow

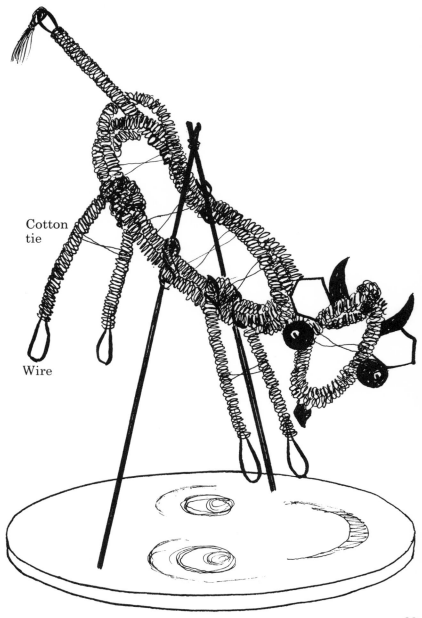

Cotton
tie

Wire

Body	cardboard tube
Eyes	shell ravioli
Legs	paper rolls with frills of tissue paper
Ears	fur
Tail	stiff paper, similar to that used for the head

Corduroy donkey

Body match box covered with corduroy velvet

Legs half clothes pegs, painted feet

Ears small metal bracelet

Eyes leather buttons

Head stuffed black stocking which also makes the neck and is pushed into end of box

Carton donkey

JANE LINTON

Made from various cartons

Neck plastic straw
Ears black card lined with white
Fringe and tail newspaper

Corrugated paper horse

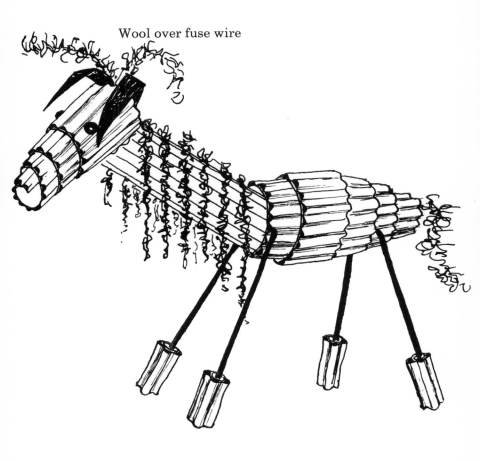

Wool over fuse wire

Corrugated paper on wire legs

Mane and tail   fluffed out
                  double-
                  knitting wool

Bonebeast

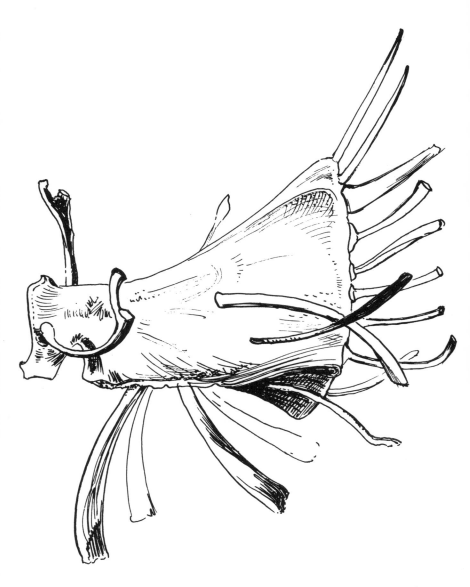

Card tube dragon

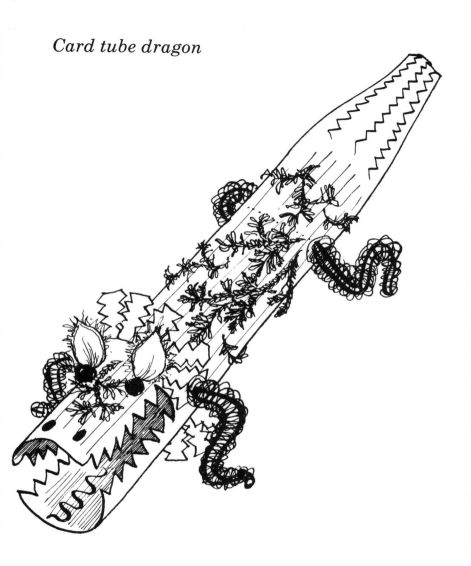

Body	white card tube from kitchen paper towel roll, painted with felt pen and decorated with pieces of cupressus
Legs	wire bound with wool

Tongue	painted
Ears	beech mast
Eyes	buttons
Tail	tapered with pinking shears

A pinked paper frill surrounds the head

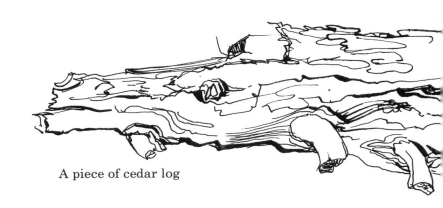

A piece of cedar log

Very old driftwood bark, light as cork

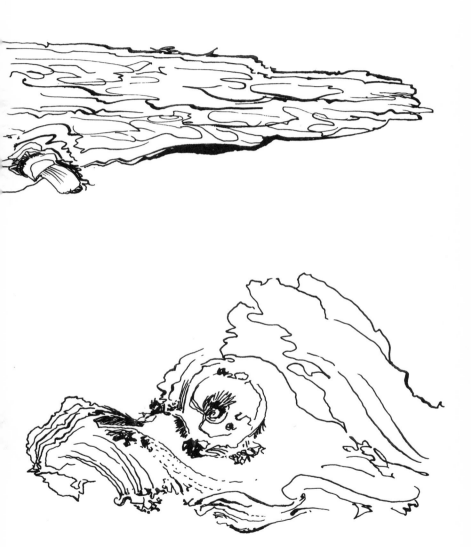

Each side suggests the head of a different animal

Skate-egg sheep

Body	dried skate eggs
Tail	catkin
Legs	cocktail *Twiglets*
Head	paper
Eyes	cloves
Mane	wool

Wire ram

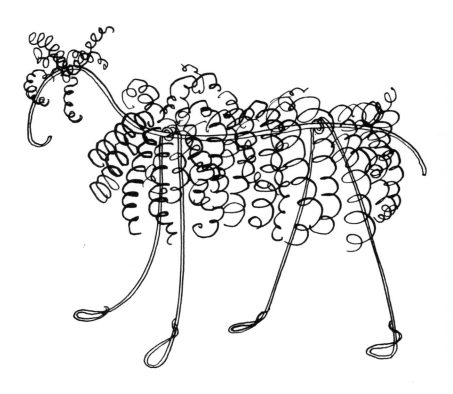

CYNTHIA CUFF

Yarn sheep

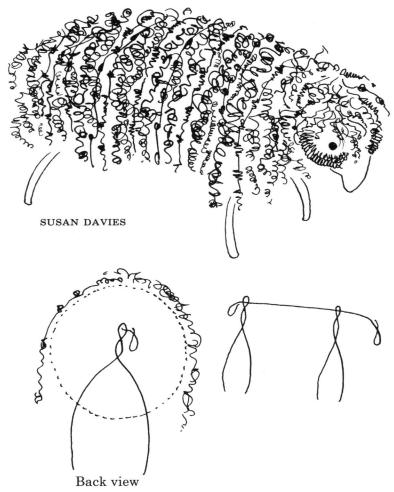

SUSAN DAVIES

Back view

Various weaving yarns over a bundle of wadding on a wire frame

Hessian sheep

Body solid roll of hessian covered with scraps of teazed hessian

Head black fabric, cut carefully and stuffed

Ears white felt

Eye bright map pin

Legs thin garden cane

Crêpe paper sheep

LESLEY BOWDEN

Crêpe paper on a wire frame
Head and feet   felt

Cartridge paper sheep

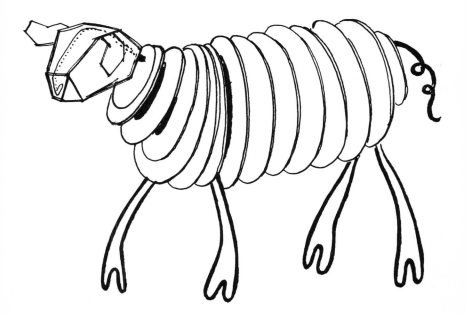

CHRISTINE HAYES

Circles of cartridge paper hung
on wire

Legs wire
Head paper

Wire frame covered with alternate rows of white tissue paper and pink cellophane

Freely tangled heavy gauge ► wire, sprayed with gold, and hung with black and gold sequins on gold lurex

Wire deer

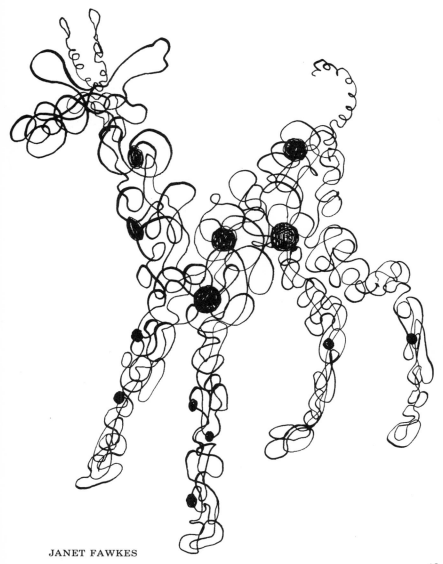

JANET FAWKES

Twisted paper snake

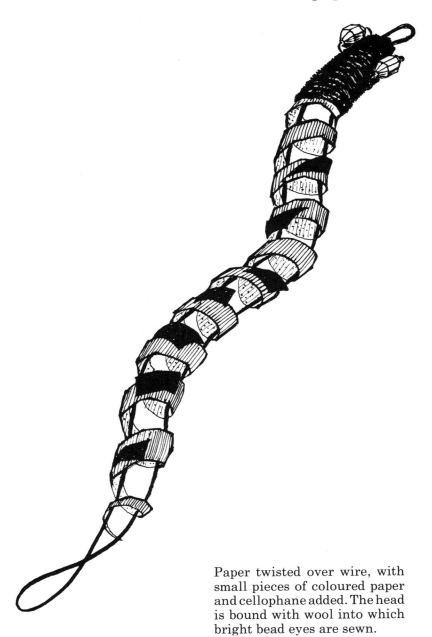

Paper twisted over wire, with
small pieces of coloured paper
and cellophane added. The head
is bound with wool into which
bright bead eyes are sewn.

Hairbrush hedgehog

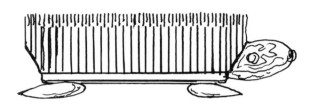

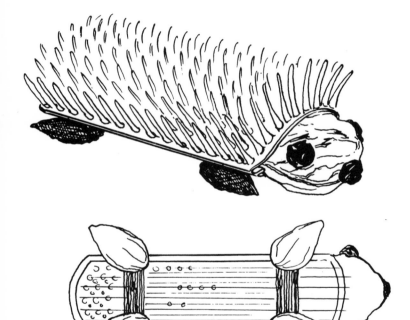

Nylon hair brush removed from handle

Head peach stone
Eyes and nose currants
Feet almonds stuck on to balsa wood gripped in place by curve of brush

Body metal pie case stuffed with paper
Head, legs and tail tightly twisted paper secured with clear gum

Stuffed towelling tortoise

Body stuffed towelling under-
          neath   chicken   wire,
          decorated with coloured
          buttons
Head, legs and tail   stuffed
          woollen glove fingers

Lemur

Body and legs heavy plaited piping cord, folded, sewn where necessary, covered with a rubber-based adhesive and bent to shape while drying

Had it been obtainable at the time, sisal rope with a wire core would have saved a good deal of trouble. The tail was made of fringed hessian squares, alternately 7 white, 7 black, threaded on plastic-covered wire, glued at intervals. Fringed hessian forms the ruff, ears, nose and eyes are felt and the pupils red faceted beads

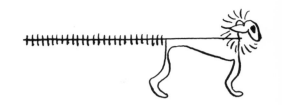

Afghan-Lemur

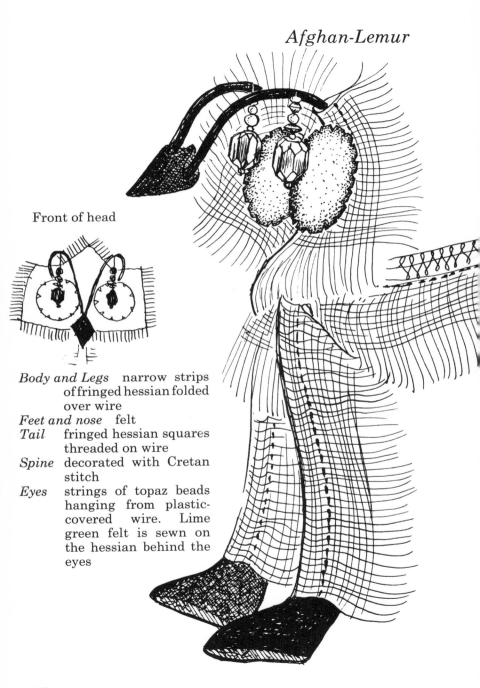

Front of head

Body and Legs narrow strips of fringed hessian folded over wire

Feet and nose felt

Tail fringed hessian squares threaded on wire

Spine decorated with Cretan stitch

Eyes strings of topaz beads hanging from plastic-covered wire. Lime green felt is sewn on the hessian behind the eyes

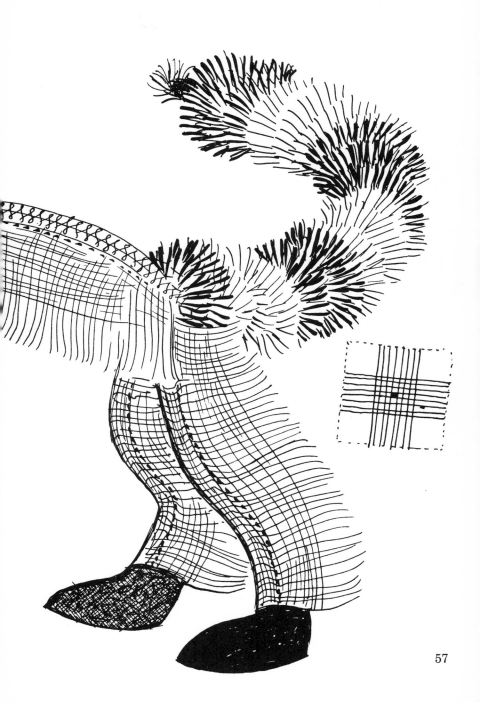

Kelp toad

Made from reverse side of fossil root

Eyes   large amber glass beads set into holes which pass through the root

When either front or back legs were added the effect of a toad was lost. The stone could be used as a head, attached to tree bark or stump and transformed into an entirely different creature

Garden monster

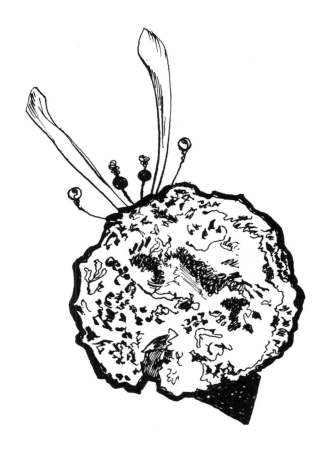

Body fossilised kelp root
Tail felt
Antennae wishbone
Eyes and feelers beads on fine
    wire embedded, with
    wishbone, in *Polyfiller*

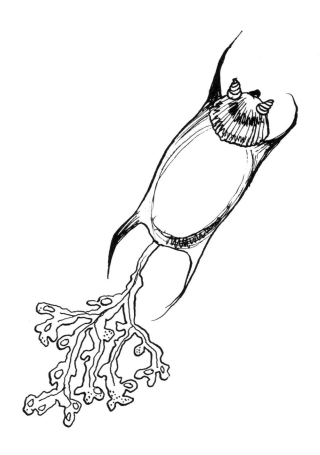

Body	skate egg case
Head	cockle shell
Eyes	tiny shells
Nose	pebble
Tail	bladder wrack seaweed

Bone iguana

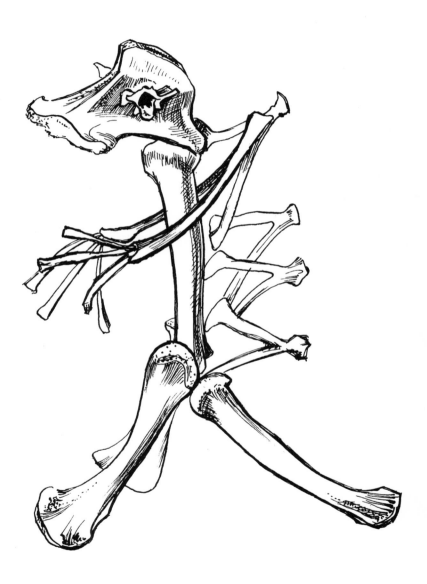

FRANCES RICHARDS

Bone dinosaur

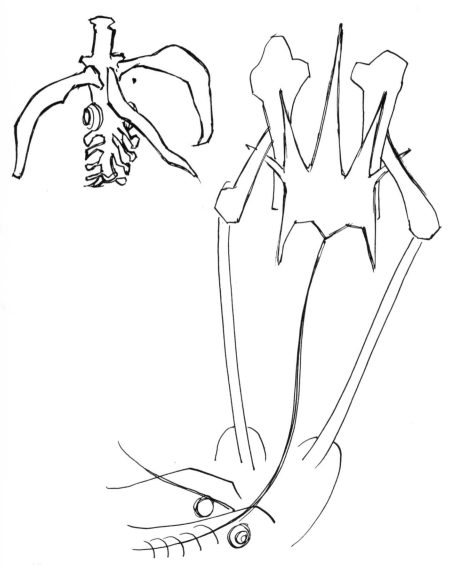

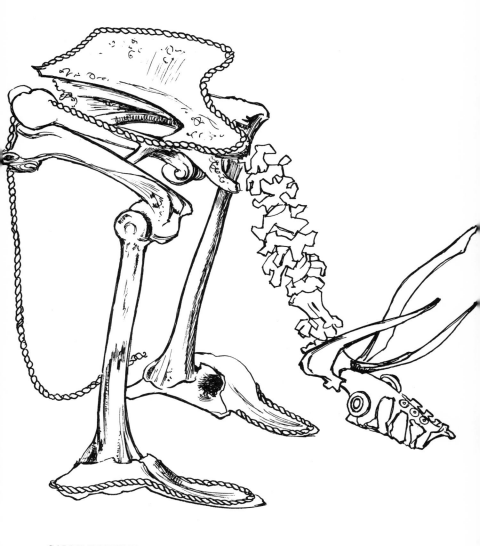

SALLY SKINNER

Bone reindeer

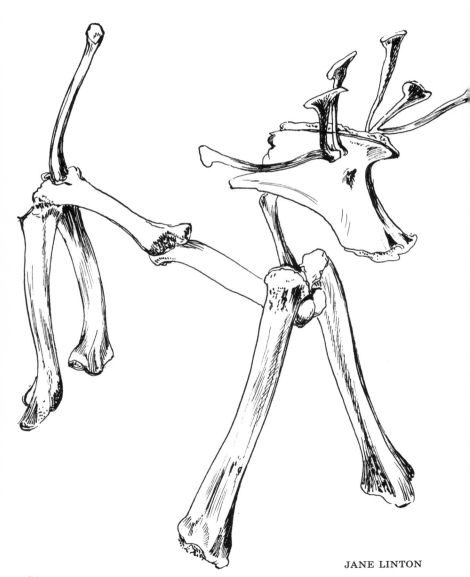

JANE LINTON

Bone dog

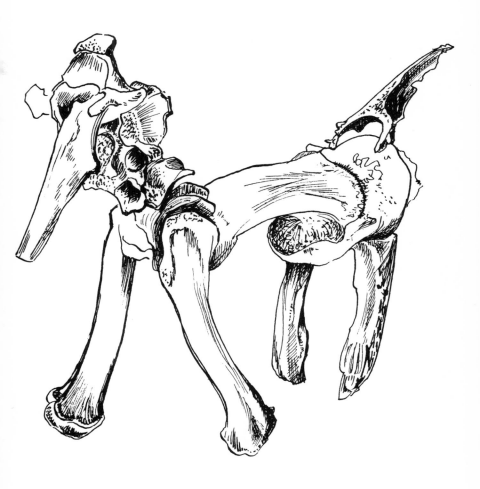

SUSAN SLADE

Metal beer bottle caps strung on firm wire. The bird stands rigidly

Bottle top peahen

Foot underneath

Foot taken through bottom of leg wire

Friendly dragon

Beer bottle caps strung on plastic-covered wire make a flexible animal

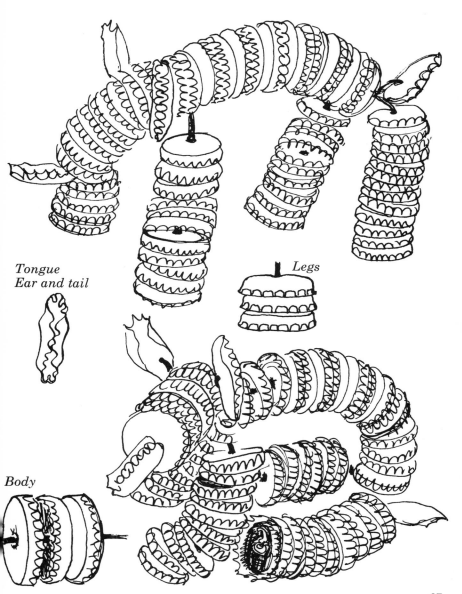

Tongue
Ear and tail

Legs

Body

Spikey dog

Body and neck rolled paper
or card tube, covered
with snipped paper
Head and feet folded felt
Legs wire from the top of a
calendar

Pipe cleaner monkey

Kangaroo

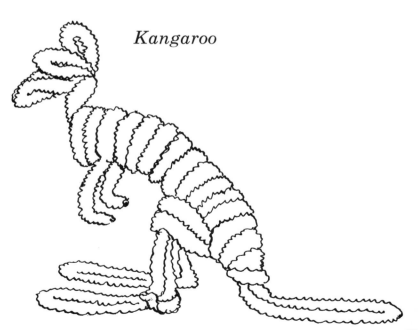

Pipe cleaner giraffe

Pipe cleaner antelope

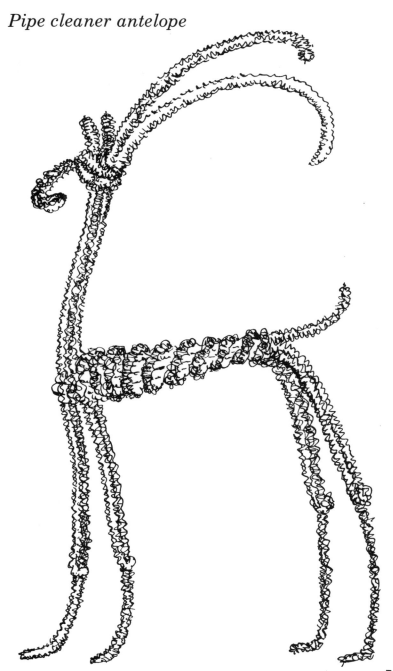

Tubal-twist dragon

Snout	bottle top set into fir cone
Eyes	white wood beads
Body	rubber handle, ping-pong balls and tin lids cut in spirals
Feet	tin lid, using the gold side uppermost

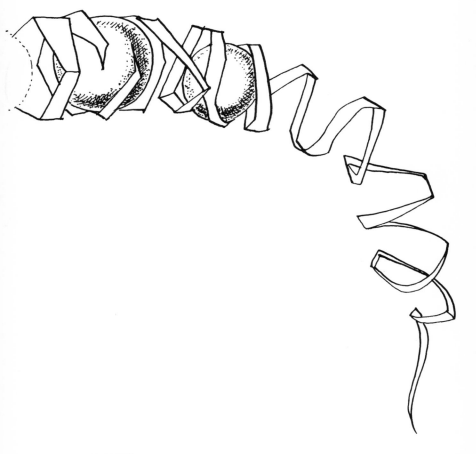

JANET FAWKES

Sycamore seed lizard

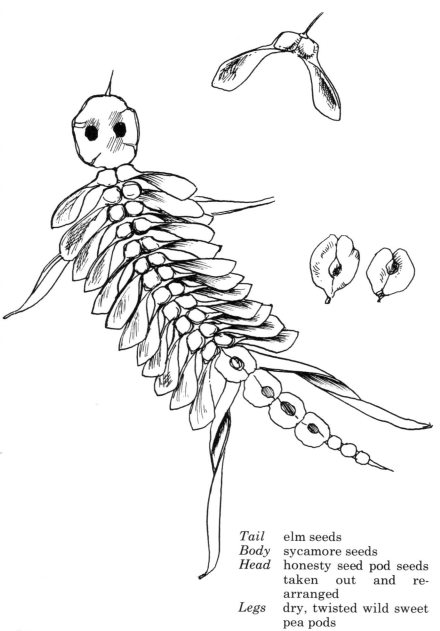

Tail	elm seeds
Body	sycamore seeds
Head	honesty seed pod seeds taken out and rearranged
Legs	dry, twisted wild sweet pea pods

Stuffed tortoise

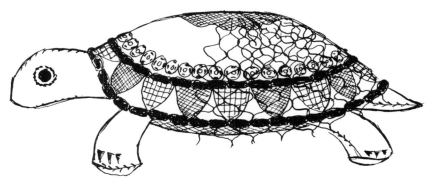

Persistence needed to make net
stick down in centre where it is
gathered and springy

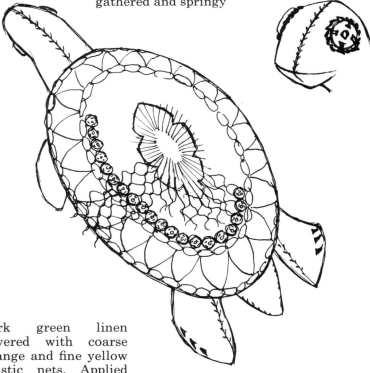

Body   dark   green   linen
covered   with   coarse
orange and fine yellow
plastic   nets.   Applied
patterned   fabric,   rug
wool and press studs
Head, feet and tail   felt

Foam rubber crocodile

Foam rubber with rust suede back

Eyes shiny black wooden beads with red-headed pin pupil

Teeth sharpened match stick chips

CATHERINE PUNNETT

Transistor alligator

Eyes   metal ring on linen
        buttons
Mouth small pieces of
        leather, tin tacks and
        tiny nails
Legs   odd screws
Body   variously striped tran-
        sistors, colours hap-
        hazardly placed, all
        mounted on core of
        tightly tangled wire

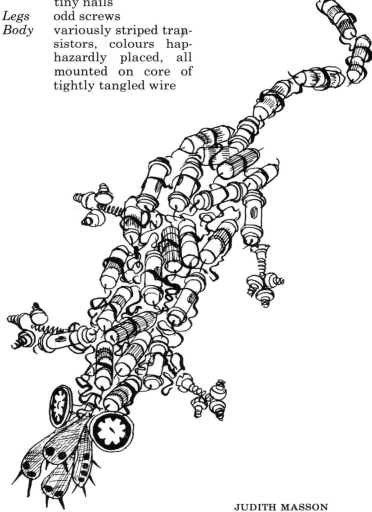

JUDITH MASSON

Seedpod llama

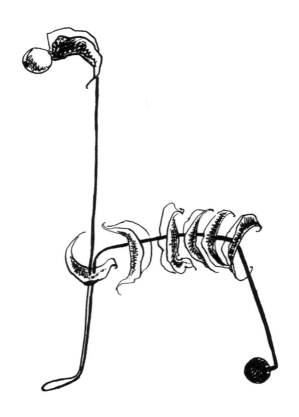

Hat wire, beads and pieces of
dried water-iris pod

Walnut snail

Body   walnut with strips of cellophane and coil of wool

Feelers fine cane and map pins

Head   folded paper

Pins stuck into thickness of card

Wool ends and tail glued between edges of shell

Card placed between edges of split walnut shell

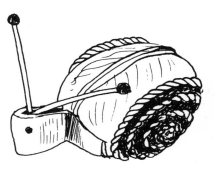

Button flies

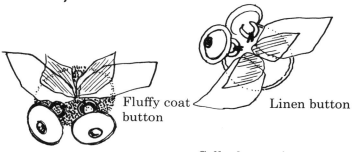

Fluffy coat button

Linen button

Cellophane wings

Sweet chestnut bees

SUSAN JARROLD

Side view

Body	a large sweet chestnut
Head	hazel nut
Wings	mottled with glue between 3 pieces of cellophane

All joined with a twist of fabric and glue

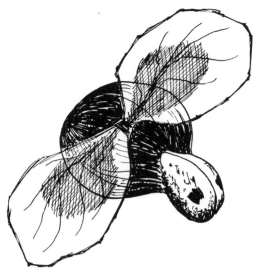

Body   large sweet chestnut
Head   dry runner bean seed

Hazel nut bee

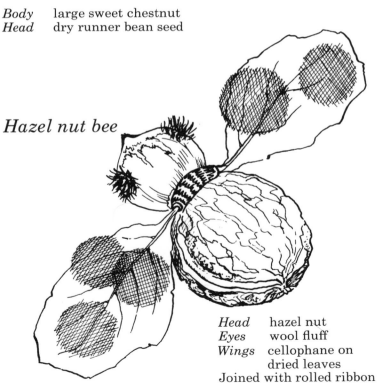

Head   hazel nut
Eyes   wool fluff
Wings   cellophane on
        dried leaves
Joined with rolled ribbon

Flying skate eggs

Body   dried skate eggs
Wings   hen feathers
Feelers budgie feathers

Spider:
Little monster from Mars

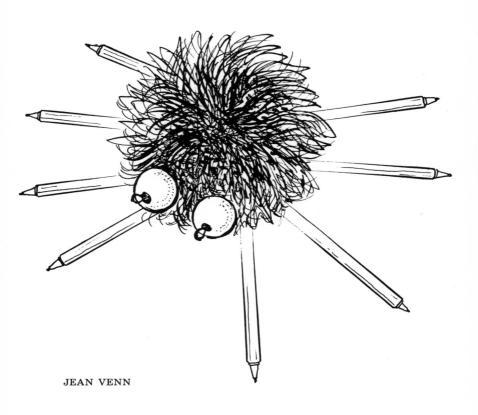

JEAN VENN

Ball point pens under a fur
pon-pon

Bead eyes

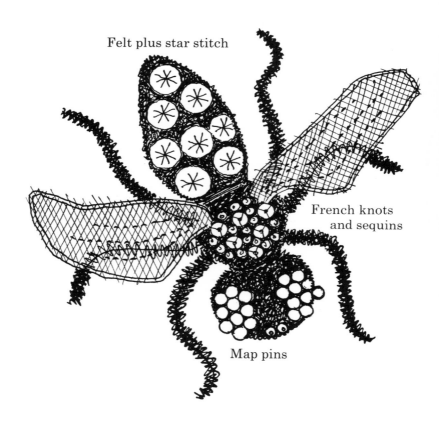

Felt plus star stitch

French knots
and sequins

Map pins

Cloth body tied with cotton

Wings wired net
Legs pipe cleaners
Eyes map pins

Crane fly

Thorax	acorn
Tail	ash twig, end sharpened, plugged into acorn and glued
Eyes	split peas on currants
Wings	hen's feathers, cut to shape and plugged into acorn
Feelers	thin feathers
Legs	copper wire

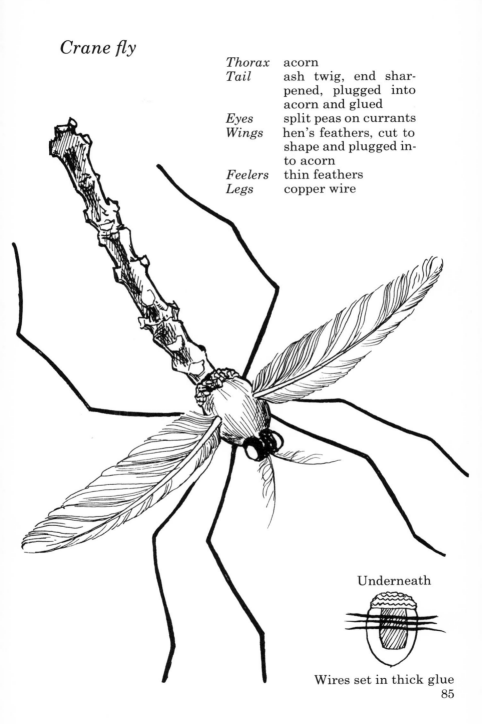

Underneath

Wires set in thick glue

Cob nut dragon fly

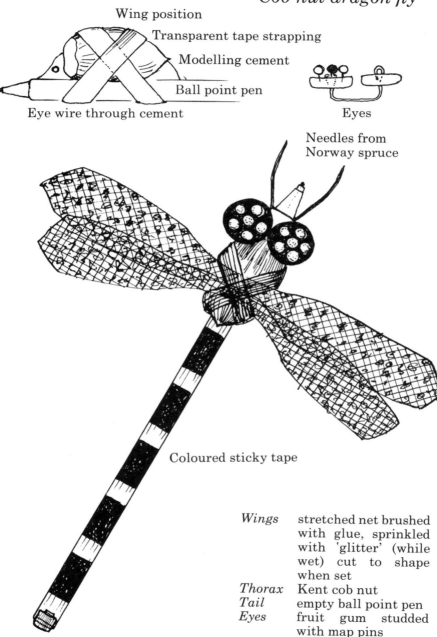

Wing position

Transparent tape strapping

Modelling cement

Ball point pen

Eye wire through cement

Eyes

Needles from
Norway spruce

Coloured sticky tape

Wings	stretched net brushed with glue, sprinkled with 'glitter' (while wet) cut to shape when set
Thorax	Kent cob nut
Tail	empty ball point pen
Eyes	fruit gum studded with map pins

Grasshopper

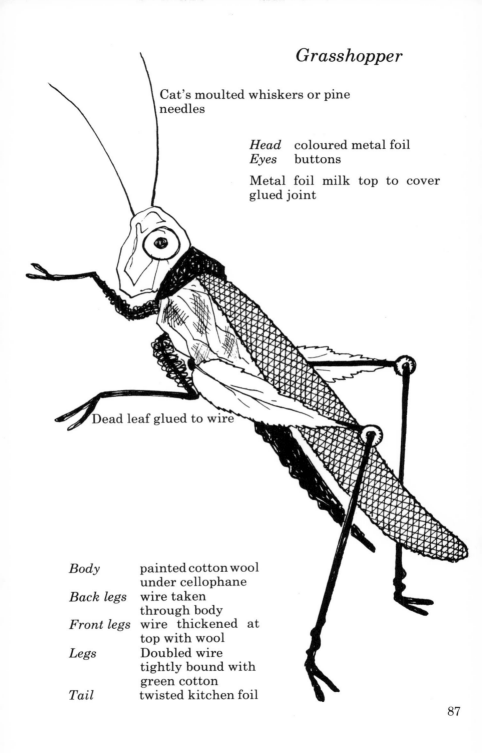

Cat's moulted whiskers or pine needles

Head   coloured metal foil
Eyes   buttons

Metal foil milk top to cover glued joint

Dead leaf glued to wire

Body   painted cotton wool
              under cellophane
Back legs   wire taken
              through body
Front legs wire thickened at
              top with wool
Legs   Doubled wire
              tightly bound with
              green cotton
Tail   twisted kitchen foil

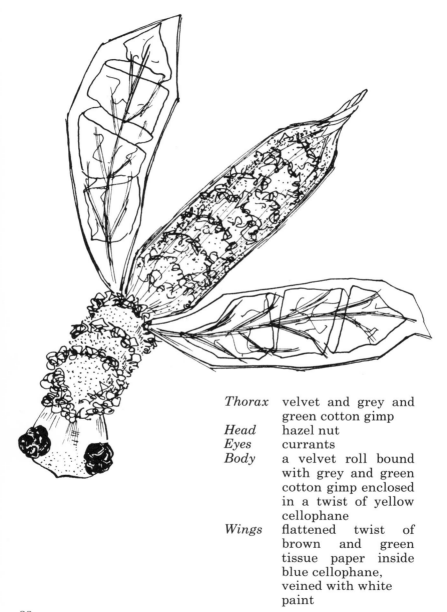

Thorax	velvet and grey and green cotton gimp
Head	hazel nut
Eyes	currants
Body	a velvet roll bound with grey and green cotton gimp enclosed in a twist of yellow cellophane
Wings	flattened twist of brown and green tissue paper inside blue cellophane, veined with white paint

Praying mantis

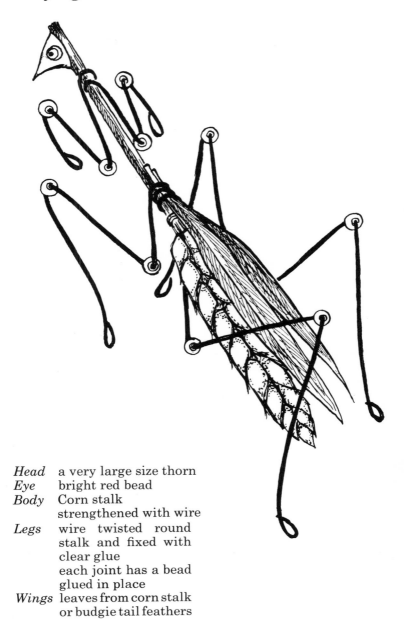

Head	a very large size thorn
Eye	bright red bead
Body	Corn stalk
	strengthened with wire
Legs	wire twisted round
	stalk and fixed with
	clear glue
	each joint has a bead
	glued in place
Wings	leaves from corn stalk
	or budgie tail feathers

Fluffy caterpillar

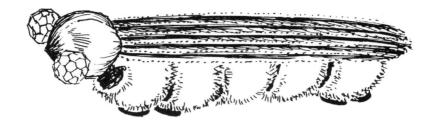

Head	hazel nut
Eyes	facetted beads
Back	cord velvet
Body	fluffy cloth over hazel nuts
Feet	felt

Looper caterpillar

Head	small cupressus cone
Body	dried peas threaded on wire
Feet	felt and rose thorns, glued on

Body and head	sticky burrs ◄
Eyes	large red berries stabbed by long coloured pins
Feelers	fuse wire
Proboscis	piece of pine needle
Wings	cellophane and fuse wire
Legs	thin copper wire, top enamelled with black

Sticky burr mosquito

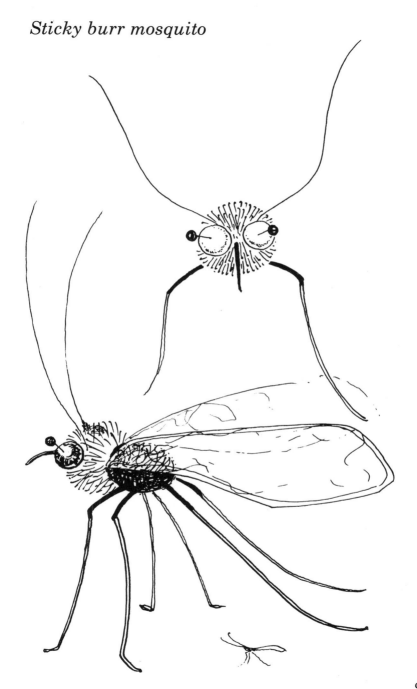

Stuffed beetles

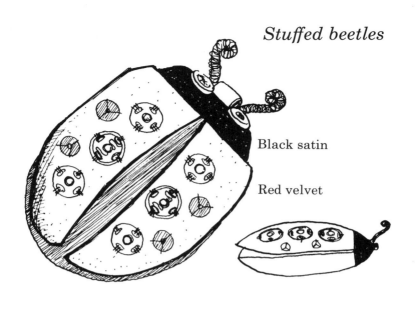

Black satin

Red velvet

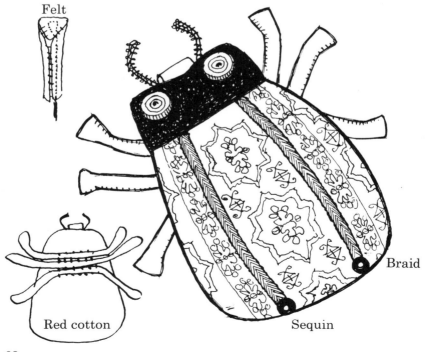

Felt

Braid

Red cotton

Sequin

Conker beetles

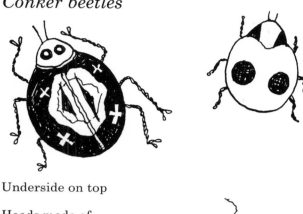

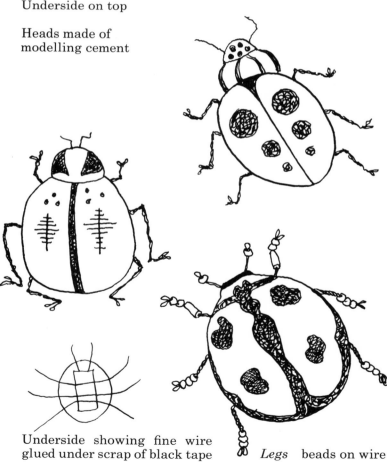

Underside on top

Heads made of
modelling cement

Underside showing fine wire
glued under scrap of black tape

Legs   beads on wire

93

Based on a cheese box – the top
cover with spotted fabric and
facetted beads

Head spotted with paint
Legs pipe cleaners
Eyes beads

Bone butterfly

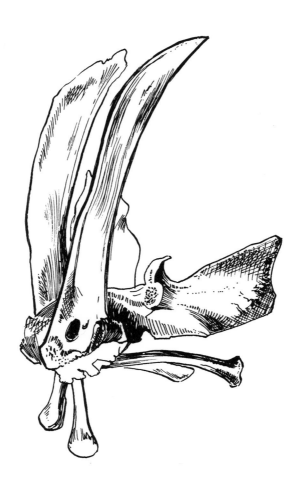

Useful materials

Assorted coloured pipe cleaners. Wire-centred sisal rope, wire in various gauges, plastic covered wire

Modelling clay: *Plasticine, Polyfiller* or some quick-drying domestic putty, or prepared putty in a tube

Modelling cement: *Alostone, Plastone*
Rubber-based adhesive: *Dufix, Evostick, Marvin Medium*
Transparent adhesive tape: *Sellotape, Scotch Tape*

Balsa wood

Coloured-headed pins, map pins, small pliers for wire, scissors for fabric and paper, pinking shears

Assorted papers: cartridge, corrugated, cellophane, crêpe, tissue, card tubes from toilet rolls and kitchen towels

Sealing foil from inside coffee tins, ends of canned fruit tins, plastic vegetable net in various sizes of mesh and colour

Ping pong balls, ball point pens, chicken wire, wire curtain spring, loofah, sponge, yoghurt cartons, beer bottle tops, milk tops, corks, bottle caps, cotton reels, screws, transistors, sealing wax, currants, cloves, cocktail sticks, cocktail biscuits (*Twiglets*), pegs, bottle brush, small boxes

Various fabrics including corduroy velvet, hessian, felt and leather scraps

Various threads, beads, buttons, sequins, lace ribbon, net, fur

Shells, pebbles, dry seaweed, dry skate eggs, cuttlefish bone, driftwood, charred wood, bark, twigs, thorns, seeds, acorns, peach stone, assorted nuts, conkers, beech mast, pine needles, feathers, fir cones, corn, straw, dried pea pods, dried berries, onions, bamboo cane, dry moss, catkins, bones